Why Animals Live in Burrows

By Valerie J. Weber

Reading consultant:

Susan Nations, M.Ed., *author/literacy coach/consultant in literacy development*

Science and curriculum consultant:

Debra Voege, M.A., *science curriculum resource teacher*

WEEKLY READER®

PUBLISHING

Please visit our web site at www.garethstevens.com.
For a free color catalog describing our list of high-quality books, call 1-800-542-2595 (USA)
or 1-800-387-3178 (Canada). Our fax: 1-877-542-2596

Library of Congress Cataloging-in-Publication Data
Weber, Valerie
　　Why animals live in burrows / by Valerie J. Weber.
　　　　p. cm. — (Where animals live)
　　Includes bibliographical references and index.
　　ISBN-10: 0-8368-8793-X　　ISBN-13: 978-0-8368-8793-8 (lib. bdg. : alk. paper)
　　ISBN-10: 0-8368-8800-6　　ISBN-13: 978-0-8368-8800-3 (softcover)
　　1. Burrowing animals—Habitations—Juvenile literature.
　I. Title.
　QL756.15.W43　2008
　591.56'48—dc22　　　　　　　　　　　　　　2007041626

This edition first published in 2008 by
Weekly Reader® Books
An Imprint of Gareth Stevens Publishing
1 Reader's Digest Road
Pleasantville, NY 10570-7000　USA

Senior Managing Editor: Lisa M. Guidone
Senior Editor: Barbara Bakowski
Creative Director: Lisa Donovan
Senior Designer: Keith Plechaty
Production Designer: Amy Ray, *Studio Montage*
Photo Researcher: Diane Laska-Swanke

Photo Credits: Cover © Joe McDonald/Corbis; pp. 1, 3 © Photodisc; p. 5 © blickwinkel/Alamy; p. 7 © Millard
H. Sharp/Photo Researchers, Inc.; pp. 8, 10 © Mattias Klum/National Geographic/Getty Images; pp. 9, 19 Diane
Blasius; p. 11 © Nigel J. Dennis/Photo Researchers, Inc.; p. 12 © Garry DeLong/Alamy; p. 13 © Jeremy O'Donnell/
Getty Images; p. 15 © Ken Lucas/Visuals Unlimited; p. 16 © Leo Keeler/Alamy; p. 17 © Michael H. Francis; p. 20 ©
Robert Clay/Alamy; p. 21 © Wim Reyns/Alamy

Printed in the United States of America

1 2 3 4 5 6 7 8 9 10 09 08 07

Table of Contents

Words that appear in the glossary are printed in **boldface** type the first time they occur in the text.

Chapter 1

A Great Place to Live

Do you sometimes want to hide from the snow, rain, or wind? Do you wish to escape the hot sun? Maybe you would like a **burrow** for a home. Many animals do.

A burrow can be as simple as a single hole in the earth. It can be a path of tunnels that stretch far underground.

Some burrows have a single tunnel with one entrance and one room. In other burrows, many entrances and tunnels lead to many rooms.

Animals have burrows for the same reasons that people have homes. Many animals bring up their babies in burrows. They keep their food there. They sleep there. Sometimes they hide from **predators** there, too.

Prairie dogs dig deep burrows with many tunnels.

Chapter 2

A Mob of Meerkats

Meerkats use their burrow homes for all those reasons. These animals live in the **grasslands** of southern Africa. As many as thirty meerkats can live in a burrow. A meerkat group is called a mob. A mob is made up of two or three families of meerkats.

Meerkats are **mammals** that are suited for digging. Their sharp, curved **claws** are like shovels. As meerkats dig, they close their ears to keep out dirt.

Meerkats have four sharp claws on each foot.

ear

claws

A meerkat's eyes have a special **membrane**. This membrane is a thin, soft sheet or layer of **tissue**. It acts like a windshield wiper. When a meerkat blinks, the membrane moves across its eye. That wipes away any sand or dirt left from digging.

Dark patches around a meerkat's eyes act like built-in sunglasses.

Meerkats dig large burrows with many tunnels. Meerkats like to make their burrows in firmly packed sand. If they dug the holes in soft sand, the burrows would fall apart easily.

Meerkats prefer to search for their food in soft sand, however. They eat fruit, worms, crickets, and other small animals.

The mound of sand around a burrow hole helps keep out rainwater.

opening

sleeping chambers

9

Each burrow has many openings above ground. The openings are both **entrances** and **exits**. Exits are handy when an enemy tries to attack the meerkats. If a predator comes in one way, the meerkats can leave through a different opening.

To a meerkat, the jackal is a dangerous predator.

At least one meerkat always guards the group and the burrow. That meerkat watches the sky for hawks or eagles. The guard also looks out for wild dogs called jackals. Those animals eat meerkats. If a predator appears, the guard barks. Then all the meerkats scurry for a hole.

A meerkat guard is always on the lookout for danger.

Meerkat burrows have many separate rooms for sleeping. These "bedrooms" can be 6 to 9 feet (2 to 3 meters) underground. They stay cool in summer and warm in winter. Meerkats cuddle close or pile on top of one another to sleep.

Meerkats huddle together inside their grass-lined burrow.

Meerkat burrows also have special rooms where mother meerkats give birth. Their babies stay in these rooms for the first few weeks of their lives. Then the young meerkats, called pups, leave the burrow with a "babysitter." A babysitter is another meerkat that cares for and protects the pups.

Meerkat pups come out of their burrow under the watchful eye of a "babysitter."

Chapter 3

Badger Burrows

Unlike meerkats, badgers usually live alone in their burrows. Only mothers with young stay together in a burrow. When the babies become adults, they go off to dig their own homes.

Badger burrows can be as deep as 10 feet (3 m) underground. They can stretch for 33 feet (10 m).

Like meerkats, badgers are good diggers. Their bodies are low and flat, with strong front legs. Their long, sharp front claws can tunnel through hard dirt. In just one minute, they can dig a hole 3 feet (1 m) deep.

Badgers have long, sharp claws suited for digging.

Most badgers dig many burrows. The animals use each one for a short time. They sleep and store food in their burrows. In winter, badgers use dirt to block the entrance to their home. Then they sleep inside for more than a day at a time.

This badger takes its prey back to its burrow.

Badgers hunt other animals that burrow, such as gophers and ground squirrels. Badgers dig their **prey** out from their burrows. Then the badgers take over those burrows. They make the prey's burrow bigger so they can live there themselves.

Badgers often borrow another animal's burrow.

Chapter 4

A Home for Many Animals

Some burrowing animals share their homes. Blue land crabs live near seashores and riverbanks. They dig burrows 6 feet (2 m) deep into the mud or sand. At the bottom of each burrow lies a small pool of water. Mosquito **larvae**, tiny fish, and other kinds of crabs live in this water. Only one blue land crab lives in a single burrow. Crabs often compete for a good spot on the shore. They will fight other crabs to protect their burrows.

Blue land crabs stay in their burrows to get away from the hot sun. The crabs usually leave their burrows only to search for food. When they return, they store food there. The burrow is like a kitchen cupboard!

This blue crab must find an empty burrow, dig a new burrow, or stay and fight to make this burrow its home.

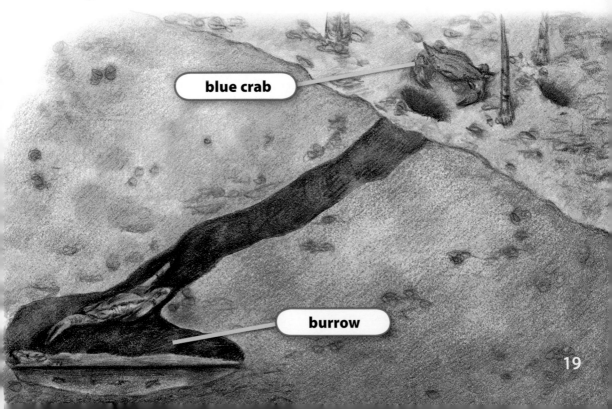

blue crab

burrow

Some animals borrow burrows instead of building their own. The tiger salamander cannot live in bright sunlight for long. During spring rains, the animal leaves its pond. The salamander hurries to a nearby squirrel burrow. It then lives there, away from the heat of the sun.

The tiger salamander cannot dig its own hole, so it finds a squirrel's burrow instead.

Burrows help animals escape heat, cold, rain, and snow. These homes protect animals, their food, and their babies. Burrows keep friends and family together and keep predators out. What more could you want from a home?

A burrow is the perfect home for this family of wild gerbils (JER-bulls).

Glossary

burrow: a hole in the ground made by an animal for shelter

claws: sharp, curved nails on the toes of animals

entrances: openings where an animal or a person goes into a place

exits: openings where an animal or a person goes out of a place

grasslands: areas covered with grasses and other short plants

larvae: very young, wingless insects, which look like worms

mammals: animals that are warm-blooded, have a backbone, and feed their babies milk made in their bodies

membrane: a thin, soft sheet or layer of tissue in the body

predators: animals that hunt and eat other animals

prey: an animal that is hunted and eaten by another animal

tissue: a layer of one kind of cells

To Find Out More

Books

Animals Under Our Feet. We Both Read (series). Sindy McKay (Treasure Bay)

Badgers. Pebble Books (series). Patricia J. Murphy (Pebble Books)

The Burrow Book. Richard Orr (DK Publishing)

Exploring Underground Habitats. Mondo's Exploring Series.
   Margaret Yatsevitch Phinney (Mondo Publishing)

Meerkats. Early Bird Nature Books (series). Conrad J. Storad
   (Lerner Publications)

Web Sites

Enchanted Learning
   www.enchantedlearning.com/coloring/Underground.shtml
   Explore burrows and the animals that live in them. You can print out fact
   sheets from this web site.

Kidport Reference Library: Animal Homes
   www.kidport.com/RefLib/Science/AnimalHomes/GroundHomes.htm
   Learn more about animals that live in burrows.

San Diego Zoo's Animal Bytes: Meerkat
   www.sandiegozoo.org/animalbytes/t-meerkat.html
   Find fun facts about meerkats and their lifestyles on the zoo's web site.

Publisher's note to educators and parents: Our editors have carefully reviewed
these web sites to ensure that they are suitable for children. Many web sites change
frequently, however, and we cannot guarantee that a site's future contents will
continue to meet our high standards of quality and educational value. Be advised
that children should be closely supervised whenever they access the Internet.

Index

About the Author

A writer and editor for more than twenty-five years, Valerie Weber especially loves working in children's publishing. Her book topics have been endlessly engaging—from the weird wonders of the sea, to the lives of girls during World War II, to the making of movies. She is grateful to her family, including her husband and daughters, and her friends for offering their support and for listening to the odd facts she has discovered during her work. Did you know, for example, that frogs use their eyeballs to push food down into their stomachs?